campusKNITS

Hey, if you're carrying around a laptop, a hand-held, or a cell phone (and who isn't?), then you need a Techno-Pouch to keep your favorite gadget looking new. How to get one? Just grab your knitting needles and some Lion Brand® yarn!

And while you're at it, fashion yourself a poncho and a pair of socks. Or make matching hoodies for yourself and a special guy. For your room, you'll love an oversized Dorm Pillow — perfect for lounging while you read or for catching a little "Z-time" before class.

Knitting is a great way to unwind, so pick your projects from these 9 campus-friendly designs, and take a break from your studies!

HOMESPUN

GAUGE for 4"x 4" (10cm x 10cm)
10 — 6mm · 20 R · 14 STS · K-10.5 6.5mm · 10 R · 10 SC

	NET		TOTAL	
	ozs	gms	yards	meters
	6	170	185	169

ACRYLIC	POLYESTER
98%	2%

CHENILLE THICK & QUICK

GAUGE for 4"x 4" (10cm x 10cm)
11 — 8mm · 16 R · 8 STS · P-15 10mm · 6.5 R · 6 SC

SOLIDS
	NET		TOTAL	
	ozs	gms	yards	meters
	–	–	100	90

PRINTS
	NET		TOTAL	
	ozs	gms	yards	meters
	–	–	75	68

ACRYLIC	RAYON
91%	9%

WOOL-EASE THICK & QUICK

GAUGE for 4"x 4" (10cm x 10cm)
13 — 9mm · 12 R · 9 STS · N-13 9mm · 8 R · 6.6 SC

	NET		TOTAL	
	ozs	gms	yards	meters
	6	170	108	97

SOLIDS, HEATHERS, TWISTS
ACRYLIC	WOOL
80%	20%

WHEAT
ACRYLIC	WOOL	RAYON
86%	10%	4%

WOOL-EASE WORSTED WEIGHT

GAUGE for 4"x 4" (10cm x 10cm)
8 — 5mm · 24 R · 18 STS · J-10 6mm · 16 R · 13.2 SC

SOLIDS, HEATHERS, TWISTS, SPRINKLES, WHEAT, MUSHROOM
	NET		TOTAL	
	ozs	gms	yards	meters
	3	85	197	180

MULTI COLORS, FROSTS, PRINTS
	NET		TOTAL	
	ozs	gms	yards	meters
	2½	70	162	146

SOLIDS, HEATHERS, TWISTS, PRINTS
WOOL	ACRYLIC
20%	80%

SPRINKLES, WHEAT, MUSHROOM
WOOL	ACRYLIC	RAYON
10%	86%	4%

MULTICOLORS
WOOL	ACRYLIC	POLYESTER
19%	78%	3%

FROSTS
WOOL	ACRYLIC	POLYESTER
20%	70%	10%

WOOL-EASE CHUNKY

GAUGE for 4"x 4" (10cm x 10cm)
10.5 — 6.5mm · 18 R · 14 STS · K-10.5 6.5mm · 11 R · 10 SC

	NET		TOTAL	
	ozs	gms	yards	meters
	5	140	153	140

SOLIDS
ACRYLIC	WOOL
80%	20%

TINSEL WHITE
ACRYLIC	WOOL	POLYESTER
78%	19%	3%

WHEAT
ACRYLIC	WOOL	RAYON
86%	10%	4%

DESIGNER: **BONNIE FRANZ**

◼◼▢▢ **EASY**

Finished Size:
 Approximately 62" x 25" [157.5 cm x 63.5 cm],
 excluding neckband

MATERIALS
 ◼ LION BRAND® Wool-Ease® Thick & Quick® **SUPER BULKY 6**
  6 balls #402 Wheat (MC)
  1 ball #404 Wood (CC)
   or colors of your choice
 ◼ Circular knitting needles, size 13 [9 mm]
  16" [40 cm], 24" [60 cm], and 36" [90 cm]
   or size needed for gauge
 ◼ LION BRAND stitch marker

GAUGE: 8.8 sts and 12 rnds = 4" [10 cm]
  in St st (k every rnd).

PONCHO

With CC and longest needle, cast on 136 sts. Place marker and join, being careful not to twist.

Work 6 rnds in K 2, P 2 Rib. Change to MC and work 13 rnds in St st.

Dec Rnd 1: *K 11, k2tog, k 12, k2tog; repeat from * to last st, k 1 - 126 sts.

Continue in St st until piece measures 17" [43 cm] from beginning.

Note: Change to shorter needles as needed.

Dec Rnd 2: *K 2, k2tog; repeat from * to last 2 sts, k 2 - 95 sts.

Work 7 rnds in St st.

Dec Rnd 3: *K 1, k2tog; repeat from * to last 2 sts, k 2 - 64 sts.

Work 7 rnds in St st.

Dec Rnd 4: *K 1, k2tog, k2tog; repeat from * to last 4 sts, k 4 - 40 sts.

Work 2 rnds in St st.

Dec Rnd 5: *K 8, k2tog; repeat from * around - 36 sts.

Change to CC. Knit 1 rnd. Work 12 rnds in K 2, P 2 Rib. Bind off loosely in rib.

DESIGNER: SARA LOUISE HARPER

◖□□□▷ **BEGINNER**

Finished Size:
   Game Board: 27" x 27" [68.5 cm x 68.5 cm]
   Bean Bag: 5" x 5" [12.5 cm x 12.5 cm]

MATERIALS

▦ LION BRAND® Wool-Ease® Chunky
   3 balls #153 Black (A)
   1 ball #140 Deep Rose (B)
   1 ball #130 Grass (C)
   1 ball #099 Fisherman (D)
      or colors of your choice
▦ LION BRAND knitting needles, size 11 [8 mm]
   or size needed for gauge
▦ LION BRAND large-eyed, blunt needle
▦ Two 4-lb. bags [3.6 kg] large dried beans

GAUGE: 12 stitches = 4" [10 cm] in
            Stockinette Stitch (knit on right side,
            purl on wrong side).

THROW

With A, cast on 81 stitches. Work 5 rows in Garter stitch (knit every row).

Next Row: Knit 4, purl 73, knit 4.

Next Row: Knit.

Repeat these 2 rows until piece measures 25½" [65 cm]. Work 5 rows in Garter stitch. Bind off.

BEAN BAGS

With B, cast on 15 stitches. Work in Stockinette stitch until piece measures 10" [25.5 cm]. Bind off. Make 4 more bags with B and 5 with C.

FINISHING
Throw

With D, embroider rows of running stitch (**Fig. 13, page 31**) as shown in diagram.

Bean Bags

Fold in half to make a 5" [12.5 cm] square and sew seam, leaving a 1" [2.5 cm] opening. Fill with beans and sew to close.

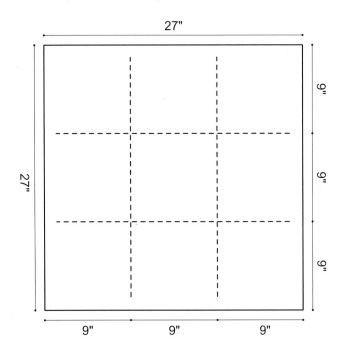

DESIGNER: **HEATHER LODINSKY**

⬤⬛☐☐ **EASY**

Finished Size: 48" x 18" [122 x 45.5 cm]

MATERIALS

▮ LION BRAND® Homespun®
     2 skeins #371 Boston Rose (A)
     2 skeins #369 Florida Keys Green (B)
     2 skeins #334 Gothic (C)
     or colors of your choice
▮ LION BRAND knitting needles, size 10 [6 mm]
     or size needed for gauge
▮ LION BRAND crochet hook,
     size K-10½ [6.5 mm]
▮ LION BRAND stitch holder
▮ 40 oz [1.1 kg] fiberfill stuffing

GAUGE: 12 sts and 20 rows = 4" [10 cm]
          in Striped Garter Stitch.

PATTERN STITCH

Striped Garter Stitch
Row 1 (RS): With A, knit.
Row 2: With A, knit.
Rows 3 and 4: With B, knit.
Rows 5 and 6: With C, knit.
Rows 7-10: With A, knit.
Rows 11-14: With B, knit.
Rows 15-18: With C, knit.
Repeat Rows 1-18 for Striped Garter Stitch.

DIAGONAL SIDE

With A, cast on 3 sts. Work in Striped Garter Stitch and, AT SAME TIME, inc 1 st at beg of every row until there are 75 sts, ending with a WS row.

Continuing in stripe pattern, dec 1 st at beg of every RS row and inc 1 st at beg of every WS row. (There should always be 75 sts after completing both rows.) Continue to work dec and inc in pattern until longer edge of work measures 48" [122 cm].

Continue in stripe pattern and dec 1 st at beg of every row until 3 sts remain. Bind off.

SHORT STRIPE SIDE

With A, cast on 54 sts. Work even in Striped Garter Stitch until piece measures 48" [122 cm]. Bind off loosely.

FINISHING

Place pieces with wrong sides together. Join C at right corner of a long edge, and single crochet through both layers around two long sides of pillow and one short side, leaving one short side open. Secure last loop with stitch holder and stuff pillow. When filled with desired amount of stuffing, place last loop on hook and single crochet opening of pillow together.

DESIGNER: **JODI LEWANDA**

◼◼◻◻ **EASY**

Finished Size: 45" x 54" [114.5 cm x 137 cm]

MATERIALS

▮ LION BRAND® Wool-Ease® Thick & Quick® **SUPER BULKY 6**
    10 balls #143 Claret (A)
    2 balls #131 Grass (B)
       or colors of your choice
▮ Circular needle, size 13 [9 mm] 29" [70 cm]
    or size needed for gauge
▮ LION BRAND stitch markers
▮ LION BRAND large-eyed, blunt needle

GAUGE: 8.75 sts and 16 rows = 4" [10 cm]
       in Seed stitch.

PATTERN STITCH

Seed stitch (multiple of 2 sts + 1)
Row 1: (K 1, p 1) across, ending k 1.
Repeat Row 1 for Seed stitch.

BLANKET STITCH

Working from left to right, bring large-eyed, blunt needle from back to front approximately ½" [13 mm] from Blanket edge. Bring needle around and from front to back through the fabric, catching yarn to form a "corner" (see diagram).

Diagram

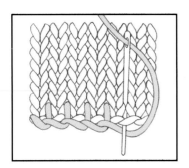

BLANKET

With A, cast on 99 sts.

Row 1 (RS): (K 1, p 1) 14 times, k 1, place marker, k 6, pm, (k 1, p 1) 14 times, k 1, pm, k 6, pm, (k 1, p 1) 14 times, k 1.

Row 2: (K 1, p 1) 14 times, k 1, slip marker, p 6, sm, (k 1, p 1) 14 times, k 1, sm, p 6, sm, (k 1, p 1) 14 times, k 1.

Row 3: (K 1, p 1) 14 times, k 1, sm, k 6, sm, (k 1, p 1) 14 times, k 1, sm, k 6, sm, (k 1, p 1) 14 times, k 1.

Repeat Rows 2-3 until piece measures 54" [137 cm]. Bind off.

POCKET

With B, cast on 43 sts. Work in St st (k on RS, p on WS) until piece measures 18" [45.5 cm]. Bind off.

FINISHING

Attach pocket on middle "panel" at bottom edge, leaving top edge open. With A, work blanket stitch across open edge of pocket. With B, work blanket stitch around entire edge of Blanket.

DESIGNER: **LISA ANNE CARNAHAN**

◼◼◻◻ **EASY**

Finished Size:
   Cell Phone: 2½" x 5" [6.5 cm x 12.5 cm]
   PDA/iPod: 3½" x 4½" [9 cm x 11.5 cm]
   Laptop: 15½" x 11½" [39.5 cm x 29 cm]

MATERIALS
◼ LION BRAND® Homespun® **BULKY 5**
   1 skein #366 Metropolis (A)
   1 skein #369 Florida Keys Green (B)
   1 skein #368 Montana Sky (C)
   1 skein #370 Coral Gables (D)
      or colors of your choice
◼ LION BRAND knitting needles, size 8 [5 mm]
      or size needed for gauge
◼ LION BRAND crochet hook, size H-8 [5 mm]
◼ Six ¾" [19 mm] black buttons
◼ Sewing needle and matching thread
◼ LION BRAND large-eyed, blunt needle

GAUGE: 14 sts = 4" [10 cm] in St st
   (k on RS, p on WS).

STITCH EXPLANATION
Ssk (slip, slip, knit) Slip next 2 sts as if to knit, one at a time, to right needle; insert left needle into fronts of these 2 sts and k them tog.

CELL PHONE
With A, cast on 9 sts.

Rows 1 and 3 (WS): K 1, *p 1, k 1; repeat from * across.

Row 2 (RS): K 1, *k 1, p 1; repeat from * to last 2 sts, k 2.

Row 4: With B, knit.

Row 5: With B, k 2, p to last 2 sts, k 2.

Row 6: With A, knit.

Row 7: With A, k 2, p to last 2 sts, k 2.

Repeat Rows 4-7 until piece measures 10" [25.5 cm] from beginning, ending with Row 7.

Work Rows 6-7 for 2 more times.

Shape Flap
Row 1: K 2, k2tog, k 1, ssk, k 2 - 7 sts.

Rows 2 and 4: K 2, p 3, k 2.

Row 3: Knit.

Row 5: K 2, k3tog, k 2 - 5 sts.

Row 6: K 2, p 1, k 2.

Row 7: K 1, k3tog, k 1 - 3 sts.

Bind off.

Instructions continued on page 15.

DESIGNER: KATHY ZIMMERMAN

■■□□ **EASY +**

Finished Size: XS (S, M, L, 1X, 2X)
Finished Chest: 36¹/₂ (40¹/₂, 43¹/₂, 47¹/₂, 50¹/₂, 54¹/₂)" [92.5 (103, 110.5, 120.5, 128.5, 138.5) cm]

Note: Pattern is written for smallest size with changes for larger sizes in parentheses. When only one number is given, it applies to all sizes. To follow pattern more easily, circle all numbers pertaining to your size before beginning.

MATERIALS
Hers
■ LION BRAND® Wool-Ease® Thick & Quick® **SUPER BULKY 6**
   4 (5, 5, 6, 6, 7) balls #106 Sky Blue (A)
   1 ball #110 Navy (B)
   2 balls #133 Pumpkin (C)
      or colors of your choice

His
■ LION BRAND® Wool-Ease® Thick & Quick® **SUPER BULKY 6**
   4 (5, 5, 6, 6, 7) balls #149 Charcoal (A)
   1 ball #106 Sky Blue (B)
   2 balls #402 Wheat (C)
      or colors of your choice

Both Hoodies
■ LION BRAND knitting needles,
   sizes 10¹/₂ [6.5 mm] and 13 [9 mm]
      or size needed for gauge
■ Circular knitting needle, size 13 [9 mm]
   24" [60 cm]
■ LION BRAND stitch markers
■ LION BRAND large-eyed, blunt needle

GAUGE: 9 sts and 12 rows = 4" [10 cm] in St st
   (k on RS, p on WS) on larger needles.

PATTERN STITCH
2 x 2 Rib (multiple of 4 sts + 2)
Row 1 (WS): P 2, *k 2, p 2; repeat from * across.
Row 2 (RS): K 2, *p 2, k 2; repeat from * across.
Repeat Rows 1-2 for 2 x 2 Rib.

NOTE
Work all increases 1 st in from edge.

BACK
With smaller needles and A, cast on 42 (46, 50, 54, 58, 62) sts.

Work in 2 x 2 Rib for 1¹/₂ (2, 2, 2, 2¹/₂, 2¹/₂)" [4 (5, 5, 5, 6.5, 6.5) cm], ending with a WS row, inc 1 st on last row - 43 (47, 51, 55, 59, 63) sts.

Change to larger needles and work even in St st until piece measures 14 (14¹/₂, 15, 15¹/₂, 16, 16¹/₂)" [35.5 (37, 38, 39.5, 40.5, 42) cm] from beg, ending with a WS row.

Shape Armholes: Bind off 4 (5, 6, 7, 8, 9) sts at beg of next 2 rows - 35 (37, 39, 41, 43, 45) sts.
Work even for 0 (2, 4, 4, 4, 6) rows.

With B, work 6 rows. With C, work even until piece measures 8 (8¹/₂, 9, 9¹/₂, 10, 10¹/₂)" [20.5 (21.5, 23, 24, 25.5, 26.5) cm] from armhole shaping, ending with a WS row.

Shape Back Neck: Work across 13 (14, 14, 15, 15, 16) sts, join 2ⁿᵈ ball of C, bind off 9 (9, 11, 11, 13, 13) sts for back neck, work across remaining 13 (14, 14, 15, 15, 16) sts.

Bind off 3 sts at each neck edge once. AT SAME TIME, bind off at shoulder edge 5 (5, 5, 6, 6, 6) sts once, then 5 (6, 6, 6, 6, 7) sts once.

 Instructions continued on page 14.

FRONT

Work as for Back until armhole shaping is completed, ending with a WS row.

Work even for 0 (2, 4, 4, 4, 6) rows.
With B, work 6 rows. With C, work 2 (2, 2, 4, 4, 6) rows.

Divide for Front Neck: Work across 15 (16, 17, 18, 19, 20) sts, place marker, k 2, join 2nd ball of C, bind off 1 st, k 2, place marker, work across remaining 15 (16, 17, 18, 19, 20) sts.

Keeping 2 sts at center neck edge in Garter stitch (k every row), work even until piece measures 6 (6½, 7, 8, 8, 8½)" [15 (16.5, 18, 20.5, 20.5, 21.5) cm] above armhole shaping, ending with a WS row.

Shape Front Neck: Work each side as follows: bind off 3 sts at center neck edge 1 (1, 2, 2, 3, 3) time(s), then 2 sts 2 (2, 1, 1, 0, 0) time(s) - 10 (11, 11, 12, 12, 13) sts remain.

Work even until piece measures same as Back to shoulders; shape shoulders as for Back.

SLEEVES

With smaller needles and A, cast on 18 (22, 22, 22, 26, 26) sts.

Work in 2 x 2 Rib for 1½ (2, 2, 2, 2½, 2½)" [4 (5, 5, 5, 6.5, 6.5) cm], ending with a WS row, inc 1 st on last row - 19 (23, 23, 23, 27, 27) sts.

Change to larger needles and St st. Inc 1 st each end every 4th row 6 (3, 5, 10, 4, 6) times, then every 6th row 3 (5, 4, 1, 5, 4) time(s) - 37 (39, 41, 45, 45, 47) sts.

Work even until piece measures 18¾ (19½, 20¾, 21½, 22½, 24)" [47.5 (49.5, 52.5, 54.5, 57, 61) cm] from beg, ending with a WS row.

Sleeve Cap: Bind off 7 (7, 8, 9, 9, 9) sts at beg of next 2 rows, then 7 (8, 8, 9, 9, 10) sts at beg of next 2 rows. Bind off remaining 9 sts.

HOOD

Sew shoulder seams. With circular needle, C, and RS facing, pick up and knit 11 (13, 13, 13, 13, 13) sts along right front neck, 15 (15, 17, 17, 19, 19) sts along back neck, 11 (13, 13, 13, 13, 13) sts along left front neck - 37 (41, 43, 43, 45, 45) sts.

Keeping first and last 2 sts in Garter stitch and working back and forth, work in St st until hood measures 11 (11½, 12, 12, 12½, 13)" [28 (29, 30.5, 30.5, 32, 33) cm]. Bind off.

FINISHING

Sew in sleeves. Sew side and sleeve seams. Sew top seam of hood.

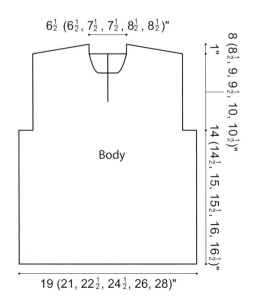

6½ (6½, 7½, 7½, 8½, 8½)"

1"

8 (8½, 9, 9½, 10, 10½)"

14 (14½, 15, 15½, 16, 16½)"

Body

19 (21, 22½, 24½, 26, 28)"

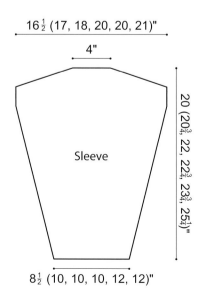

16½ (17, 18, 20, 20, 21)"

4"

20 (20¾, 22, 22¾, 23¾, 25¼)"

Sleeve

8½ (10, 10, 10, 12, 12)"

PDA/iPOD

With A, cast on 13 sts.

Rows 1 and 3 (WS): K 1, *p 1, k 1; repeat from * across.

Row 2 (RS): K 1, *k 1, p 1; repeat from * to last 2 sts, k 2.

Row 4: With C, knit.

Row 5: With C, k 2, p to last 2 sts, k 2.

Row 6: With A, knit.

Row 7: With A, k 2, p to last 2 sts, k 2.

Repeat Rows 4-7 until piece measures 9" [23 cm] from beginning, ending with Row 7.

Work Rows 6-7 for 2 more times.

Shape Flap
Rows 1, 3 and 5: K 2, k2tog, k to last 4 sts, ssk, k 2.

Rows 2, 4 and 6: K 2, p to last 2 sts, k 2.

Row 7: K 2, k3tog, k 2 - 5 sts.

Bind off.

LAPTOP

With A, cast on 55 sts.

Rows 1 and 3 (WS): K 1, *p 1, k 1; repeat from * across.

Row 2: K 1, *k 1, p 1; repeat from * to last 2 sts, k 2.

Row 4: With D, knit.

Row 5: With D, k 2, p to last 2 sts, k 2.

Row 6: With A, knit.

Row 7: With A, k 2, p to last 2 sts, k 2.

Repeat Rows 4-7 until piece measures 23" [58.5 cm] from beginning, ending with Row 7.

Work Rows 6-7 for 4 more times.

Shape Flap
Rows 1 and 3: K 2, k2tog, k to last 4 sts, ssk, k 2.

Row 2: K 2, p2tog tbl, p to last 4 sts, p2tog, k 2 - 51 sts.

Row 4: K 2, p to last 2 sts, k 2.

Repeat Rows 1-4 until 7 sts remain, ending with Row 4.

Next Row: K 2, k3tog, k 2 - 5 sts.

Bind off.

FINISHING

For each Pouch, sew 1 button on flap and 1 button on Pouch. Crochet a 5" [12.5 cm] chain and attach to underside of flap under button. Fold in half and sew side seams.

DESIGNER: ELENA MALO

◼◼◻◻ **EASY +**

Finished Size:
Hat: 20" [51 cm] circumference
Mittens: 8" [20.5 cm] around fingers;
10" [25.5 cm] long
Scarf: 6" x 60" [15 cm x 152.5 cm]

MATERIALS
▮ LION BRAND Wool-Ease® Chunky **BULKY 5**
2 balls #152 Charcoal (A)
1 ball #099 Fisherman (B)
1 ball #146 Orchid (C)
or colors of your choice
▮ LION BRAND knitting needles, size 11 [8 mm]
or size needed for gauge
▮ LION BRAND knitting needles,
size 10½ [6.5 mm]
▮ LION BRAND stitch markers
▮ LION BRAND stitch holder
▮ LION BRAND large-eyed, blunt needle
▮ Tassel maker (optional)

GAUGE: 12½ sts and 18 rows = 4" [10 cm]
in St st (k on RS, p on WS) on larger
needles.

NOTE
Fasten off each color at the end of each stripe.
Weave in tails as you work by catching tail in first
6 sts of next row, tacking it to WS.

HAT
With larger needles and A, cast on 75 sts.

Row 1 (RS): P 1, (k 1, p 1) across.

Row 2: K 1, (p 1, k 1) across.

Repeat Rows 1-2 for rib for 12 rows total.

Change to smaller needles and continue in rib until
piece measures 5" [12.5 cm], ending with a WS
row.

Dec Row: K 5, (k2tog, k 5) across - 65 sts.

Purl one row. Change to St st and work even in
stripe pattern as follows: 2 rows B, 2 rows A, 6
rows C, (2 rows A, 2 rows B) 2 times.

Shape Crown:
Row 1: K 2, (k2tog, k 5) across - 56 sts.

Row 2 and all WS rows: Purl.

Row 3: K 2, (k2tog, k 4) across - 47 sts.

Row 5: K 2, (k2tog, k 3) across - 38 sts.

Row 7: K 2, (k2tog, k 2) across - 29 sts.

Row 9: K 1, (k2tog) across - 15 sts.

Row 10: P 1, (p2tog) across - 8 sts.

Fasten off, leaving a 20" [51 cm] tail.

Instructions continued on page 21.

17

DESIGNER: LISA ANNE CARNAHAN

■■■☐ INTERMEDIATE

Finished Size: Adult M (L)
Circumference: 8 (9)" [20.5 (23) cm]

Note: Pattern is written for smaller size with changes for larger size in parentheses. When only one number is given, it applies to both sizes. To follow pattern more easily, circle all numbers pertaining to your size before beginning.

MATERIALS
■ LION BRAND® Wool-Ease®
  1 ball #170 Peacock (A)
  1 ball #140 Rose Heather (B)
  1 ball #139 Dark Rose Heather (C)
    or colors of your choice
■ LION BRAND double-pointed needles,
    size 8 [5 mm] or size needed for gauge
■ LION BRAND stitch markers
■ LION BRAND large-eyed, blunt needle

GAUGE: 20 sts and 28 rows = 4" [10 cm]
    in St st (k every rnd).

STITCH EXPLANATIONS
Ssk (slip, slip, knit): Slip next 2 sts as if to knit, one at a time, to right needle; insert left needle into fronts of these 2 sts and k them tog.
Kitchener Stitch (Grafting): Holding the 2 needles parallel with wrong sides of fabric together, thread a large-eyed, blunt needle with one of the yarn ends and work as follows:

Insert needle as if to purl into first stitch on front piece. Insert needle as if to knit into first stitch on back piece. Then follow steps 1-4 as outlined below. 1) Insert needle as if to knit through first st on front needle and let the st drop from needle. 2) Insert needle into 2nd st on front needle as if to purl and pull the yarn through, leaving st on the needle. 3) Insert needle into first st on back needle as if to purl and let it drop from the needle, then 4) insert it as if to knit through 2nd st on back needle and pull the yarn through, leaving st on needle. Repeat steps 1-4 until all sts are gone. When finished, adjust tension as necessary.

CUFF
With A, loosely cast on 40 (44) sts. Divide sts onto 3 double-pointed needles. Place marker and join, being careful not to twist. Work in K 1, P 1 Rib for 1" [2.5 cm].

With B, knit 4 rnds.

With C, knit 4 rnds.

Repeat these 8 rnds until leg measures approximately 7" [18 cm] from beginning, ending with 4 rnds of B.

Instructions continued on page 20.

HEEL FLAP

With A, k 10 (11), slip remaining sts to next needle (this needle will hold the instep sts); turn work.

Next Row: P 10 (11) and then p 10 (11) from next needle; slip remaining sts to instep needle.

There should be 20 (22) sts on each of 2 needles. Work back and forth on the heel stitches only.

Row 1 (RS): *Slip 1, k 1; repeat from * across.

Row 2 (WS): Slip 1, purl across.

Repeat Rows 1 and 2 until heel flap measures 2¹/₄" [5.5 cm], ending with Row 2.

TURN HEEL

Row 1: Slip 1, k 10 (12), ssk, k 1; turn - 19 (21) sts.

Row 2: Slip 1, p 3 (5), p2tog, p 1; turn - 18 (20) sts.

Row 3: Slip 1, k 4 (6), ssk, k 1; turn - 17 (19) sts.

Row 4: Slip 1, p 5 (7), p2tog, p 1; turn - 16 (18) sts.

Row 5: Slip 1, k 6 (8), ssk, k 1; turn - 15 (17) sts.

Row 6: Slip 1, p 7 (9), p2tog, p 1; turn - 14 (16) sts.

Row 7: Slip 1, k 8 (10), ssk, k 1; turn - 13 (15) sts.

Row 8: Slip 1, p 9 (11), p2tog, p 1; turn - 12 (14) sts.

Pick up and knit stitches for heel gusset as follows: With A, knit 6 (7) sts; place end of rnd marker; with C, knit 6 (7) sts, pick up and knit 11 sts along edge of heel flap, place first marker; knit 20 (22) sts of instep, place second marker; pick up and knit 11 sts along edge of heel flap, knit remaining 6 (7) sts - 54 (58) sts.

GUSSET

Continue working 4 rnd stripe pattern as established and at same time work gusset as follows:

Rnd 1: Knit.

Rnd 2: Knit to 3 sts before first marker, k2tog, k 1; slip marker, knit to second marker, slip marker, k 1, ssk; knit to end of rnd.

Repeat Rnds 1 and 2 until 40 (44) sts remain.

Note: Keep markers in place for toe shaping.

FOOT

Work even in St st stripe pattern until foot measures 7¹/₂ (8¹/₂)" [19 (21.5) cm], or 2" [5 cm] less than desired total length.

TOE

Rnd 1: With A, knit to 3 sts before first marker, k2tog, k 1; slip marker, k 1, ssk, knit to 3 sts before second marker, k2tog, k 1; slip marker, k 1, ssk, knit to end of rnd.

Rnd 2: Knit.

Repeat Rnds 1 and 2 until 16 (20) sts remain.

Knit across first 4 (5) sts of rnd. 8 (10) sts will be for the top of foot and 8 (10) sts will be for the bottom of foot. Using Kitchener stitch, graft remaining stitches together, grafting top of foot to bottom of foot.

FINISHING

Thread tail through remaining sts, pull tight to gather, and fasten securely. Sew side seam, reversing seam 3" [7.5 cm] from lower edge for cuff of Hat. With C, make a 4" [10 cm] tassel, winding yarn 25 times around tassel maker or 4" [10 cm] piece of cardboard. Attach tassel to top of Hat.

MITTENS

With smaller needles and A, cast on 33 sts. Work 12 rows in K 1, P 1 Rib as for Hat.

Change to larger needles and St st and work even in stripe pattern as follows: (2 rows A, 2 rows B) 5 times.

Keeping to stripe pattern, work next row as follows: K 13, place next 7 sts on stitch holder, k 13 - 26 sts.

Work even for a total of 14 stripes from rib, ending with a stripe of B. *With A, k 13, slip remaining 13 sts onto holder. Bind off 2 sts at beginning of next 4 rows, bind off remaining 5 sts. Repeat from * with remaining 13 sts on holder.

Thumb:

With larger needles and C, cast on 1 st, k 7 sts from holder, cast on 1 st - 9 sts. Work 10 rows in St st.

Dec Row: (K2tog) across - 5 sts.
Fasten off, leaving a 7" [18 cm] tail.

FINISHING

Thread tail through remaining sts, pull tight to gather, and fasten securely. Sew thumb seam. Sew side and top seams.

SCARF

With larger needles and A, cast on 18 sts. Work 12 rows in Garter st (k every row).

Continue in Garter st stripe pattern as follows:
*(4 rows B, 4 rows A) 8 times, 12 rows C; repeat from * 2 more times, then work (4 rows B, 4 rows A) 7 times, 4 rows B, 12 rows A. Bind off all sts.

With C, make 4 tassels as for hat. Attach a tassel to each corner.

DESIGNER: JODI LEWANDA

◼◼◻◻ **EASY**

Finished Size: Approximately 8¹/₂" x 10¹/₂" x 2¹/₂"
[21.5 cm x 26.5 cm x 6.5 cm]

MATERIALS
◼ LION BRAND® Wool-Ease® Thick & Quick® **SUPER BULKY 6**
    2 balls #114 Denim (MC)
    1 ball #099 Fisherman (CC1)
    or colors of your choice
◼ LION BRAND Chenille Thick & Quick **SUPER BULKY 6**
    1 skein #189 Wine (CC2)
    or color of your choice
◼ LION BRAND knitting needles, size 13 [9 mm]
    or size needed for gauge
◼ LION BRAND large-eyed, blunt needle

GAUGE: With MC, 10 sts and 20 rows = 4" [10 cm]
in Garter st (k every row).

EMBROIDERY NOTES
Running Stitch: Thread needle and pass it in and
out of the knitted piece, making the surface stitches
and spaces of equal length.

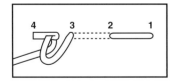

Lazy Daisy Stitch: Thread needle and bring from
back to front through knitted piece (base of petal).
*Insert needle as closely as possible to base of
petal, then bring needle back up at tip of petal.
Loop the yarn under the needle. Pull needle away
from you. Insert needle into knitted piece just over
the looped yarn. Take needle to the back to anchor
the stitch. Repeat from * for each petal.

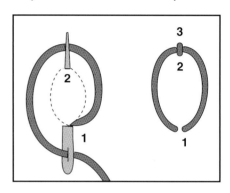

French Knot: Thread needle and bring from back to
front through knitted piece. Wrap yarn around
needle 3 times and insert needle back into knitted
piece just next to where it came up from back.
Holding wrapped yarn in place on needle, pull
needle through to back. Tighten knot.

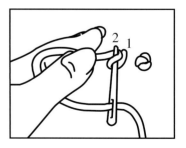

Continued on page 24.

FRONT

With MC, cast on 22 sts.

Work in Garter st until piece measures 10½"
[26.5 cm]. Bind off.

BACK

With MC, cast on 22 sts.

Work in Garter st until piece measures 10½"
[26.5 cm], ending with a WS row.

Flap

Next Row (RS): P2tog, purl to last 2 sts, p2tog -
20 sts.

Work 2" [5 cm] in Garter st, ending with a WS row.

Next Row (RS): Purl.
Work 4" [10 cm] in Garter st. Bind off.

SIDE AND STRAP

With MC, cast on 6 sts.

Work in Garter st until piece measures 48"
[122 cm]. Bind off.

ASSEMBLY

Sew short ends of strap together, being careful not
to twist length.
Pin strap to Bag front, centering strap seam at
bottom and easing corners. Sew in place along side
and bottom edges.
Pin back piece to strap and front, centering strap
seam at bottom and easing corners. Sew in place
along side and bottom edges.

EMBROIDERY

With CC2, embroider "daisies" on flap using Lazy
Daisy stitch.
With CC1, embroider running stitch around bag
front, back and flap. Add random French Knots on
flap.

ABBREVIATIONS

beg = begin(ning)
CC = Contrasting Color
cm = centimeters
dec = decreas(e)(s)(ing)
inc = increas(e)(s)(ing)
k = knit
k2tog = knit 2 together
k3tog = knit 3 together
MC = Main Color
mm = millimeters
p = purl
pm = place marker
p2tog = purl 2 together
rnd(s) – round(s)
RS = right side
sm = slip marker
ssk = slip, slip, knit
st(s) = stitch(es)
St st = Stockinette stitch
tbl = through back loop
tog = together
WS = wrong side

* — When you see an asterisk used within a
   pattern row, the symbol indicates that
   later you will be told to repeat a portion
   of the instruction. Most often the instructions
   will say, repeat from * so many times.
** or *** — Used to set off a block of text. Look
   for the direction, repeat between **'s and
   ***'s so many times.
( ) or [ ] — Set off a short number of stitches that
   are repeated or indicated additional
   information.

GAUGE

Never underestimate the importance of gauge.
Achieving the correct gauge assures that the
finished size of your piece matches the finished
size given in the pattern.

CHECKING YOUR GAUGE

Work a swatch that is at least 4" (10 cm) square.
Use the suggested needle size and the number of
stitches given. For example, the standard Lion
Brand® Wool-Ease® Thick & Quick® gauge is:
9 sts + 12 rows = 4" (10 cm) on size 13 (9 mm)
needles. If your swatch is larger than 4" (10 cm),
you need to work it again using smaller needles; if
it is smaller than 4" (10 cm), try it with larger
needles. This might require a swatch or two to get
the exact gauge given in the pattern.

METRICS

As a handy reference, keep in mind that 1 ounce =
approximately 28 grams and 1" = 2.5 centimeters.

TERMS

continue in this way or as established — Once a
pattern is set up (established), the instructions my
tell you to continue in the same way.

fasten off — To end your piece, you need to simply
pull the yarn through the last loop left on the
needle. This keeps the last stitch intact and prevents
the work from unraveling.

right side — Refers to the front of the piece.

work even — This is used to indicate an area
worked as established without increasing or
decreasing.

wrong side — Refers to the back of the piece.

25

KNIT TERMINOLOGY	
UNITED STATES	**INTERNATIONAL**
gauge =	tension
bind off =	cast off
yarn over (YO) =	yarn forward (yfwd) **or**
	yarn around needle (yrn)

Yarn Weight Symbol & Names	SUPER FINE **1**	FINE **2**	LIGHT **3**	MEDIUM **4**	BULKY **5**	SUPER BULKY **6**
Type of Yarns in Category	Sock, Fingering Baby	Sport, Baby	DK, Light Worsted	Worsted, Afghan, Aran	Chunky, Craft, Rug	Bulky, Roving

KNITTING NEEDLES															
U.S.	0	1	2	3	4	5	6	7	8	9	10	10½	11	13	15	17
U.K.	13	12	11	10	9	8	7	6	5	4	3	2	1	00	000	---
Metric - mm	2	2.25	2.75	3.25	3.5	3.75	4	4.5	5	5.5	6	6.5	8	9	10	12.75

●□□□ **BEGINNER**	Projects for first-time knitters using basic knit and purl stitches. Minimal shaping.
●■□□ **EASY**	Projects using basic stitches, repetitive stitch patterns, simple color changes, and simple shaping and finishing.
●■■□ **INTERMEDIATE**	Projects with a variety of stitches, such as basic cables and lace, simple intarsia, double-pointed needles and knitting in the round needle techniques, mid-level shaping and finishing.
●■■► **EXPERIENCED**	Projects using advanced techniques and stitches, such as short rows, fair isle, more intricate intarsia, cables, lace patterns, and numerous color changes.

BASIC KNIT STITCHES & TECHNIQUES

MARKERS

As a convenience to you, we have used markers to help distinguish the beginning of a pattern. Place markers as instructed. You may use purchased markers or tie a length of contrasting color yarn around the needle. When you reach a marker on each row, slip it from the left needle to the right needle; remove it when no longer needed.

KNITTING IN THE ROUND

Using a circular needle, cast on all stitches as instructed. Untwist and straighten the stitches on the needle before beginning the first round.

Place a marker after the last stitch to mark the beginning of a round. Hold the needle so that the ball of yarn is attached to the stitch closest to the **right** hand point.

To begin working in the round, knit the stitches on the left hand point (**Fig. 1a**).

Fig. 1a

Continue working each round as instructed **without turning the work**; but for the first three rounds or so, check to be sure that the cast on edge has not twisted around the needle. If it has, it is impossible to untwist it. The only way to fix this is to rip it out and return to the cast on row.

When working a project that is too small to use a circular needle, or the size circular needle is unavailable in the length needed, double-pointed needles are required. Divide the stitches into thirds or fourths and slip $1/3$ or $1/4$ of the stitches onto each of the double-pointed needles, forming a triangle or square. With the last needle, knit across the first needle (**Fig. 1b**). You will now have an empty needle with which to knit the stitches from the next needle. Work the first stitch of each needle firmly to prevent gaps.

Fig. 1b

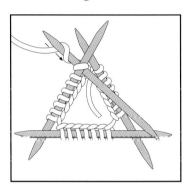

ZEROS

To consolidate the length of an involved pattern, Zeros are sometimes used so that all sizes can be combined. For example, increase every sixth row 5 [1, 0] time(s) means the first size would increase 5 times, the second size would increase one, and the largest size would do nothing.

HINTS

As in all pieces, good finishing techniques make a big difference in the quality of the piece. Do not tie knots. Always start a new ball at the beginning of a row, leaving ends long enough to weave in later.

GARTER STITCH

Knit every row. Two rows of knitting make one horizontal ridge in your fabric *(Fig. 2)*.

Fig. 2

SEED STITCH

Seed Stitch is a reversible fabric that doesn't curl at the edges. Alternate the knit and purl stitches on the first row. On the following rows, knit the purl stitches and purl the knit stitches as they face you *(Fig. 3)*.

Fig. 3

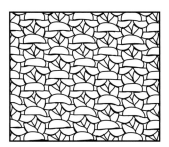

STOCKINETTE STITCH

Knit one row or number of stitches indicated (right side), purl one row or number of stitches indicated. The knit side is smooth and flat *(Fig. 4a)*, and the purl side is bumpy *(Fig. 4b)*.

Fig. 4a

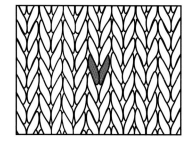

Fig. 4b

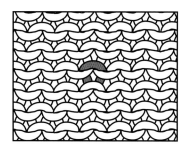

REVERSE STOCKINETTE STITCH

Reverse Stockinette Stitch is worked the same as Stockinette Stitch with the exception that the purl side of your fabric is considered to the the right side.

DECREASES
KNIT 2 TOGETHER (abbreviated k2tog)

Insert the right needle into the front of the first two stitches on the left needle as if to knit (**Fig. 5**), then knit them together as if they were one stitch.

Fig. 5

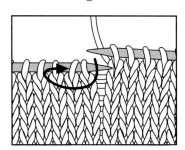

PURL 2 TOGETHER (abbreviated p2tog)

With yarn held in front of work, insert the right needle into the front of the first two stitches on the left needle as if to purl (**Fig. 6**), then purl them together as if they were one stitch.

Fig. 6

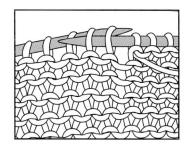

KNIT 3 TOGETHER (abbreviated k3tog)

Insert the right needle into the front of the first three stitches on the left needle as if to knit (**Fig. 7**), then **knit** them together as if they were one stitch.

Fig. 7

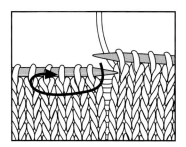

SLIP, SLIP, KNIT (abbreviated ssk)

Slip next two sts as if to knit, one at a time, to right needle; insert left needle into fronts of these two sts and knit them together (**Figs. 8a-c**).

Fig. 8a

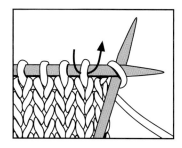

Fig. 8b

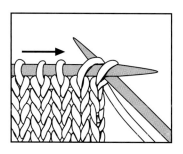

Fig. 8c

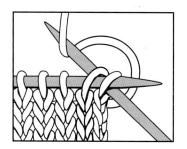

KNIT INCREASE

Knit the next stitch but do not slip the old stitch off the left needle *(Fig. 9a)*. Insert the right needle into the back loop of the same stitch and knit it *(Fig. 9b)*, then slip the old stitch off the left needle.

Fig. 9a

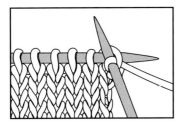

Fig. 9b

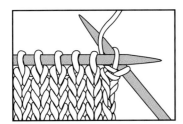

PICKING UP STITCHES

When instructed to pick up stitches, use one of the needles and the yarn that you are going to continue working with. Insert your knitting needle from the **front** to the **back** under two strands at the edge of the worked piece *(Figs. 10a & b)*. Wrap the yarn around the needle as if to **knit**, then bring the needle with the yarn back through the stitch to the right side, resulting in a stitch on the needle. Repeat this along the edge.

Fig. 10a

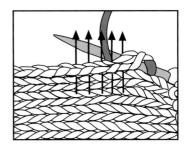

Fig. 10b

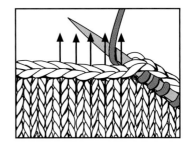

EMBROIDERY STITCHES

LAZY DAISY STITCH

Thread needle and bring from back to front through knitted piece (base of petal). *Insert needle as closely as possible to base of petal, then bring needle back up at tip of petal. Loop the yarn under the needle. Pull needle away from you. Insert needle into knitted piece just over the looped yarn. Take needle to the back to anchor the stitch. Repeat from * for each petal **(Fig. 11)**.

Fig. 11

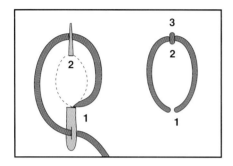

FRENCH KNOT

Bring the needle up at 1. Wrap yarn around the needle once and insert the needle at 2, holding end of yarn with non-stitching fingers **(Fig. 12)**. Tighten knot; then pull needle through, holding the yarn until it must be released.

Fig. 12

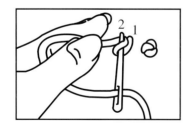

RUNNING STITCH

Thread needle and pass it in and out of the knitted piece, making the surface stitches and spaces of equal length **(Fig. 13)**.

Fig. 13

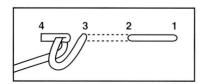

BASIC CROCHET STITCHES

CHAIN

To work a chain, begin with a slip knot on the hook. Bring the yarn **over** hook from back to front, catching the yarn with the hook and turning the hook slightly toward you to keep the yarn from slipping off. Draw the yarn through the slip knot **(Fig. 14)**.

Fig. 14

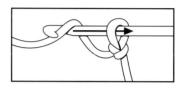

SLIP STITCH

To work a slip stitch, insert hook in stitch or space indicated, yo and draw through stitch or space and through loop on hook **(Fig. 15)**.

Fig. 15

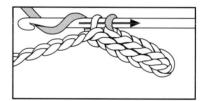

SINGLE CROCHET

Insert hook in stitch indicated, yo and pull up a loop, yo and draw through both loops on hook **(Fig. 16)**.

Fig. 16

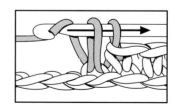

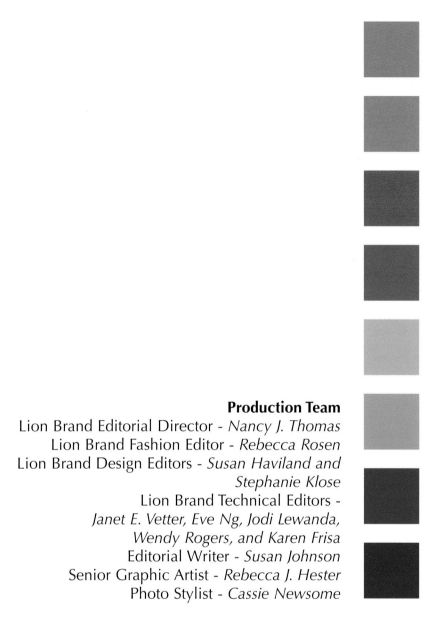

Production Team
Lion Brand Editorial Director - *Nancy J. Thomas*
Lion Brand Fashion Editor - *Rebecca Rosen*
Lion Brand Design Editors - *Susan Haviland and Stephanie Klose*
Lion Brand Technical Editors - *Janet E. Vetter, Eve Ng, Jodi Lewanda, Wendy Rogers, and Karen Frisa*
Editorial Writer - *Susan Johnson*
Senior Graphic Artist - *Rebecca J. Hester*
Photo Stylist - *Cassie Newsome*

We have made every effort to ensure that these instructions are accurate and complete.
We cannot, however, be responsible for human error, typographical mistakes, or variation in individual work.

PRINTED WITH SOYINK

Made in U.S.A.